SECRETS OF THE ANIMAL WORLD

KANGAROOS
Animals with a Pouch

by Andreu Llamas
Illustrated by Gabriel Casadevall and Ali Garousi

Gareth Stevens Publishing
MILWAUKEE

BP

For a free color catalog describing Gareth Stevens' list of high-quality books and multimedia programs, call 1-800-542-2595 (USA) or 1-800-461-9120 (Canada). Gareth Stevens Publishing's Fax: (414) 225-0377. See our catalog, too, on the World Wide Web: http://gsinc.com

The editor would like to extend special thanks to Jan W. Rafert, Curator of Primates and Small Mammals, Milwaukee County Zoo, Milwaukee, Wisconsin, for his kind and professional help with the information in this book.

Library of Congress Cataloging-in-Publication Data

Llamas, Andreu.
   [Canguro. English]
   Kangaroos: animals with a pouch / by Andreu Llamas; illustrated by Gabriel Casadevall and Ali Garousi.
      p. cm. — (Secrets of the animal world)
   Includes bibliographical references and index.
   Summary: Describes the physical characteristics, habitat, behavior, and life cycle of these large marsupials.
   ISBN 0-8368-1637-4 (lib. bdg.)
   [1. Kangaroos—Juvenile literature. 2. Kangaroos.] I. Casadevall, Gabriel, ill. II. Garousi, Ali, ill. III. Title. IV. Series.
QL737.M35L5313   1997
599.2'22—dc21   96-46916

This North American edition first published in 1997 by
Gareth Stevens Publishing
1555 North RiverCenter Drive, Suite 201
Milwaukee, Wisconsin 53212 USA

This U.S. edition © 1997 by Gareth Stevens, Inc. Created with original © 1993 Ediciones Este, S.A., Barcelona, Spain. Additional end matter © 1997 by Gareth Stevens, Inc.

Series editor: Patricia Lantier-Sampon
Editorial assistants: Diane Laska, Rita Reitci

Printed in the United States of America

1 2 3 4 5 6 7 8 9 01 00 99 98 97

CONTENTS

AN ISOLATED WORLD

Where kangaroos live

Kangaroos live mainly in Australia, one of the most unique regions of the world. Both the animals and the flora of this remote country are very different from the rest of the world. Australia is a very large country (over 2.7 million square miles (7 million sq. kilometers), and the special evolution of its species is due to its isolation, surrounded by water like an island, since the Tertiary period 50 million years ago. For this reason, Australia is home to mammals that have evolved in a very different way from those throughout the rest of the world.

The first scientists to see the kangaroo could hardly believe their eyes.

Australia and some nearby islands are the natural habitat of kangaroos, which live in both jungle and desert regions.

The astounding marsupial

Kangaroos are marsupials, a group that includes a wide variety of animals — from desert rats and squirrels to animals that look like wolves. While marsupial species live in the Americas, most live in Australia, New Guinea, and a few nearby islands.

The characteristic shared by all marsupials is that the female of the species has a pouch, or marsupium, in which the offspring develop. The pouch also contains mammary glands, which give milk.

The koala is an Australian marsupial that looks like a cuddly toy bear.

Types of kangaroos

About 35 species and 90 subspecies of kangaroos exist. Some have the same build as an average-size human, and others are smaller than rats.

Kangaroos belong to the scientific family Macropodidae, which means "of large feet," because their hind legs are bigger than their forelimbs.

Some kangaroos live in steamy rain forests, others in deserts, and some species can be found almost everywhere in Australia.

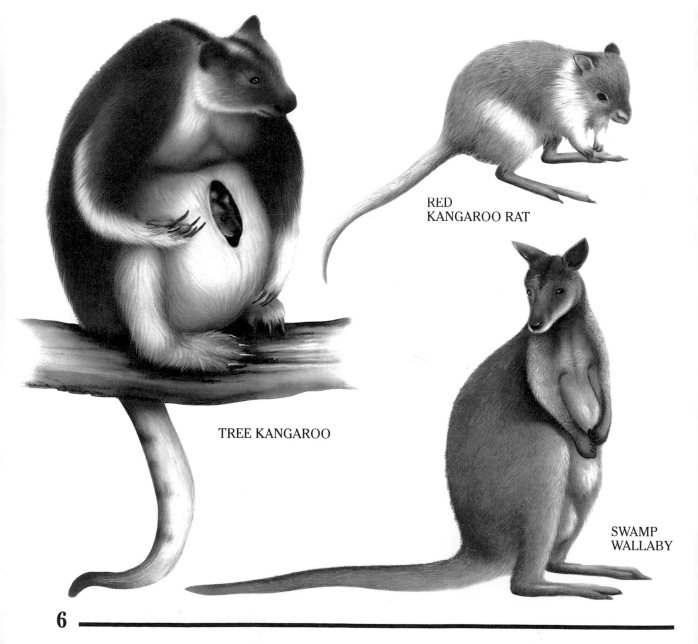

TREE KANGAROO

RED KANGAROO RAT

SWAMP WALLABY

ROCK WALLABY

TAMMAR
WALLABY

RED KANGAROO

Kangaroos are plant-eaters, or herbivores, although the specific diet may vary from species to species. Macropodidae vary in appearance and size, so they are classified into three groups: *1)* quokkas, which measure 12 inches (30 centimeters) in length and weigh around 18 ounces (500 grams); *2)* the kangaroo rats, whose sizes vary between that of a rabbit and a rat; and *3)* typical kangaroos and wallabies. Tree kangaroos are also included in this group.

INSIDE THE KANGAROO

The kangaroo is very similar to other mammals: its skin is covered with hair, it has four limbs (two forelegs and two hind ones), and the female (called a doe) has mammary glands to feed her offspring milk.

But the kangaroo is also a marsupial. Females of the species have a special pouch around the abdomen. This is the main feature that distinguishes it from other mammals. The pouch is used to nurture, carry, and protect young.

This illustration shows what the best-known marsupial species looks like both on the outside and the inside.

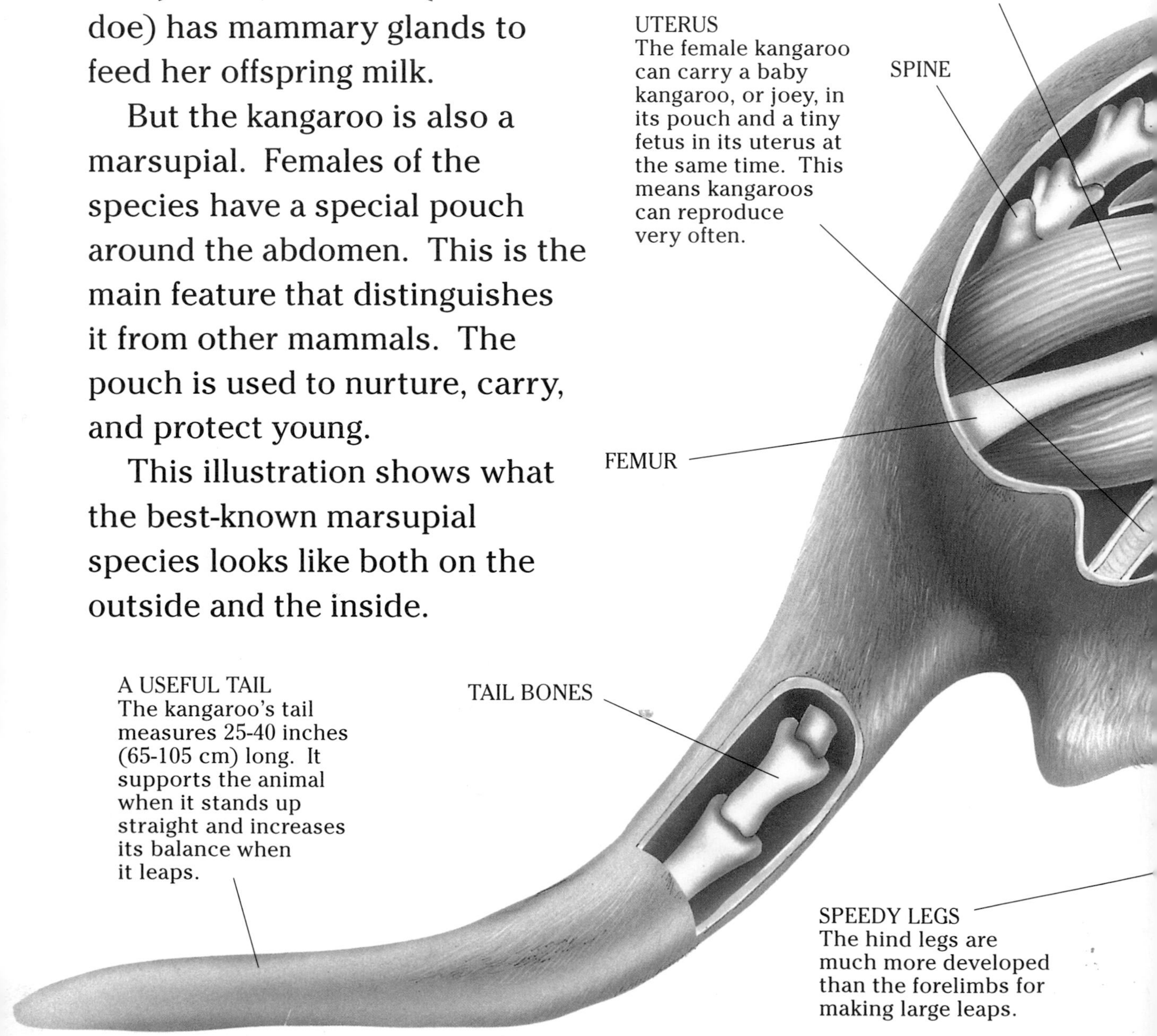

MUSCLES
Limb muscles are so powerful that the kangaroo can jump up to 10 feet (3 m) high.

UTERUS
The female kangaroo can carry a baby kangaroo, or joey, in its pouch and a tiny fetus in its uterus at the same time. This means kangaroos can reproduce very often.

SPINE

FEMUR

A USEFUL TAIL
The kangaroo's tail measures 25-40 inches (65-105 cm) long. It supports the animal when it stands up straight and increases its balance when it leaps.

TAIL BONES

SPEEDY LEGS
The hind legs are much more developed than the forelimbs for making large leaps.

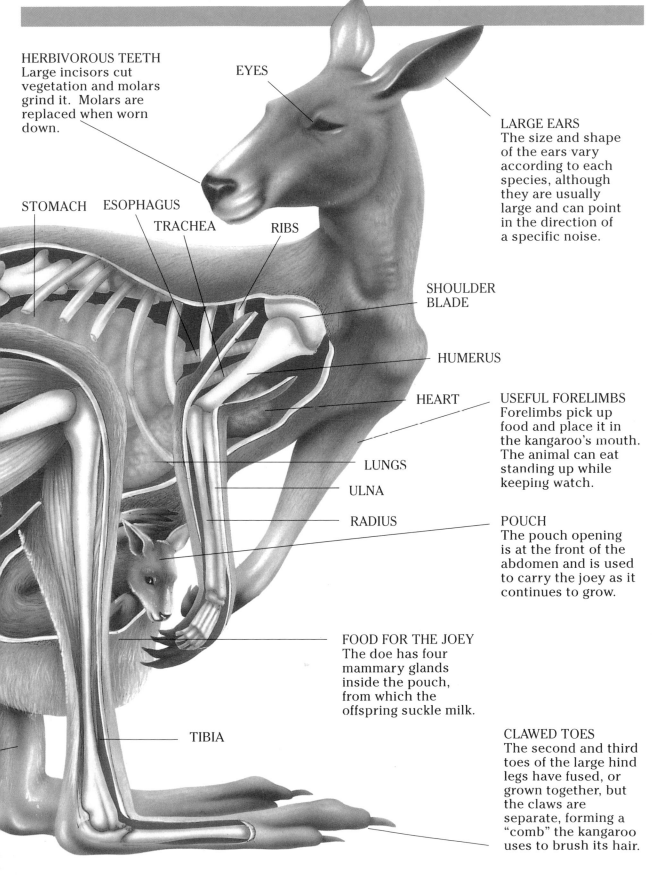

HERBIVOROUS TEETH
Large incisors cut vegetation and molars grind it. Molars are replaced when worn down.

EYES

LARGE EARS
The size and shape of the ears vary according to each species, although they are usually large and can point in the direction of a specific noise.

STOMACH

ESOPHAGUS

TRACHEA

RIBS

SHOULDER BLADE

HUMERUS

HEART

USEFUL FORELIMBS
Forelimbs pick up food and place it in the kangaroo's mouth. The animal can eat standing up while keeping watch.

LUNGS

ULNA

RADIUS

POUCH
The pouch opening is at the front of the abdomen and is used to carry the joey as it continues to grow.

FOOD FOR THE JOEY
The doe has four mammary glands inside the pouch, from which the offspring suckle milk.

TIBIA

CLAWED TOES
The second and third toes of the large hind legs have fused, or grown together, but the claws are separate, forming a "comb" the kangaroo uses to brush its hair.

ANIMALS WITH A POUCH

The marsupium

The marsupial's pouch, or marsupium, varies in size and appearance according to each species. Some marsupials do not even have a pouch; the banded anteater, also called a numbat, is one species that lacks a pouch. When the numbat's offspring are born, normally three or four at a time, they remain attached to the matted hair covering the mother's stomach. Then they cling permanently to the mother's mammary glands.

In other species, the pouch is only a fold in the skin of the stomach. But in the best-known marsupials, such as the kangaroo, the marsupium forms a pouch in which the offspring

The joey travels around with its mother inside the pouch until it is four months old, when it weighs about 6.5 to 9 pounds (3 to 4 kg).

can be protected. The shape of the pouch may also vary.

Quadruped marsupials, such as wombats, walk on all fours and have their pouch opening at the back to keep it as clean as possible while making tunnels. The kangaroo's pouch opening is at the front. If kangaroos walked on all fours, their offspring would tumble out.

A young bandicoot climbs into its mother's pouch from behind.

Wombats build very complex networks of tunnels.

Koala pouches open from below, and joeys have to cling tightly not to fall. Older joeys travel on the mother's back.

An incredible journey

The marsupium is the pouch where the joey spends its first months of life. Gestation lasts between thirty and forty days. Twenty-four hours before the birth, the doe lies down on her two hind legs with her tail laid out on the ground between her legs. Then she inserts her head into the pouch and cleans it with her tongue.

Like all marsupials, the kangaroo is born in an under-developed state. It weighs less than .04 ounce (1 g) and is about the size of a bee. At birth, the offspring's eyes and ears do not work, and it does not have hair.

Guiding itself by smell, the newborn, still attached by its umbilical cord, climbs up its mother's abdomen. After about fifteen minutes, the offspring makes it into the pouch, goes to one of the four nipples, and begins to suckle. The small creature clings tightly and will not let go until it is time to leave the pouch about 200 days later.

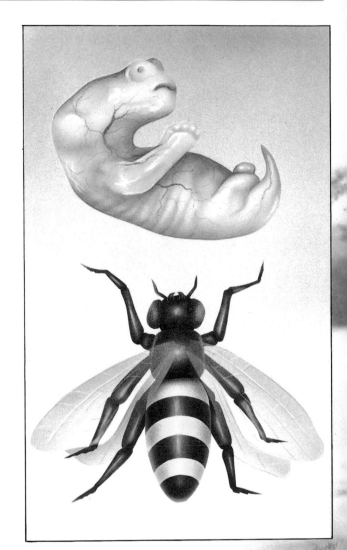

A newborn kangaroo compared to a bee for size.

The baby kangaroo must climb its mother's abdomen to reach the pouch.

Once inside the pouch, the joey clings tightly to one of the nipples.

THE LIFE OF A KANGAROO

Traveling in a pouch

By about two hundred days old, the joey is totally covered with hair and begins to leave the pouch to explore the outside world. The first few excursions last only for minutes at a time, but they gradually get longer.

The joey dives head first into the pouch, swings itself around inside, and sticks its head out.

The joey likes to travel with its head outside its mother's pouch.

If the kangaroo troop moves or if danger approaches, the joey can dive into the pouch and swing its body around so that its head is thrust out of the pouch. When the joey gets larger, sometimes even the hind legs and tail are also left sticking out.

At the age of four months, the kangaroo weighs 6.5 to 9 pounds (3 to 4 kg). Now it travels outside the pouch. But it continues to suckle by putting its head inside the pouch until it is one year old. Sometimes the young kangaroos want to enter the pouch even when they are too big. The mother keeps them from trying by holding them back with her arms.

When the joey is slightly bigger, it may sometimes still stick its head inside the pouch.

Running and jumping

When a kangaroo moves as part of a troop, and while feeding, it can travel about 8 miles (13 km) an hour by jumping in 6.5-foot (2-m) leaps. To eat, the kangaroo leans forward on its hind legs, with its front legs touching the ground.

To escape danger, the kangaroo jumps at great speed. The way it moves is totally different from other quadrupeds. The kangaroo uses its hind legs with its feet together, although normally one foot is several inches (cm) behind the other. The forelimbs are folded up under the animal's chest and help balance the kangaroo.

The weight of the kangaroo's tail counterbalances the weight of the animal's body.

When a kangaroo is being chased, it can jump distances of 30 feet (9 m) in length and over 10 feet (3 m) in height and can reach speeds of 30 miles (50 km) an hour.

The kangaroo's large tail remains stretched out and helps balance it when it jumps.

When the kangaroo grazes, it moves slowly and uses its four limbs and tail to support itself.

When it is chased, it can move 30 miles (50 km) an hour, jumping with its tail stretched out.

The kangaroo can jump up to 10 feet (3 m) high and 30 feet (9 m) long.

Did You Know...?

that there are tree kangaroos?

Some species of kangaroos, called dendrolages, have adapted to life in the trees. They measure between 20 to 32 inches (50 to 80 cm), not including the tail, and they all have strong front legs and sharp claws for gripping branches. The tree kangaroos spend most of their lives in the treetops eating fruit, leaves, and twigs, although they occasionally descend to the ground.

KANGAROO ANCESTORS

Marsupials of the past

About 100 million years ago, marsupials inhabited most continents. Marsupial fossils of various ages have been found in Australia and the Americas. As other animals evolved more quickly, the marsupials were gradually confined to small areas, until only ninety species survived in the Americas. These marsupials were about the size of the opossum. Marsupials arrived in Australia about 50 million years ago, when it was still joined to Asia. For millions of years, the marsupial was able to spread and diversify into hundreds of species, since there was no competition. Now about 200 marsupial species inhabit the Australia-New Guinea region.

The kangaroo's ancestor was the enormous Procoptodon, which measured up to 10 feet (3 m) in height.

About 30,000 years ago, Thylacoleus carnifex, the marsupial lion, inhabited the Australian continent.

that there were
saber-toothed marsupials?

Between 5 and 10 million years ago, a powerful marsupial predator roamed the forests of South America. It was called *Thylacosmilus*, and its body was 6.5 feet (2 m) long. It looked like a lion and had two sharp, curved, canine teeth projecting from its upper jaw. This carnivorous marsupial became extinct when it had to compete with other, more evolved carnivores arriving from North America about 5 million years ago.

KANGAROO SURVIVAL

Natural enemies

For millions of years, before humans and their animals arrived, kangaroos had few enemies. The marsupial wolf and the long-tailed eagle sometimes hunted joeys and, in tropical regions, crocodiles and snakes also caught kangaroos.

When humans arrived in Australia from southern Asia about 12,000 years ago, they brought dogs with them. These dogs eventually became a wild species. The dingo, as this dog is called, is Australia's most important predator today.

Because of their small size, wallabies are easy prey for the dogs and foxes that were introduced to Australia by the early settlers.

The dingo is a feared predator.

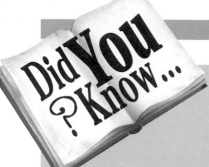

that kangaroos dig wells?

Some kangaroos live in areas where long droughts are common. Although they eat plants containing water, they still need to drink at least once a day. To cope with these dry conditions, kangaroos sometimes dig wells in dry riverbeds, and the holes can be 3 feet (1 m) deep. Because of these wells, other animals such as emus, pigeons, and cockatoos also have a means of survival.

Fighting kangaroos

Kangaroos rarely fight among themselves. Fights only take place over the females during mating. The kangaroos stand on their hind legs and scratch each other and try to grab each other's forelimbs. One may lean back on its tail or a rock or tree and give its rival a powerful kick in the stomach. The kangaroo uses these techniques against other enemies, too. It can also jump into the water when being chased by a dog. The kangaroo lets the predator reach the water, then holds the dog's head under water until it drowns.

Using its tail as a support, the kangaroo can kick its opponent with its hind legs.

Kangaroos scratch and pull at their enemies.

APPENDIX TO

KANGAROOS
Animals with a Pouch

KANGAROO SECRETS

▼ **The red kangaroo is the biggest of all.** It can measure over 9 feet (2.8 m) from its snout to the tip of its tail.

▼ **The Tasmanian devil.** This marsupial is an active predator measuring 2-3 feet (60-90 cm). It can be found only on the island of Tasmania. In spite of

its name, it can be tamed. Then it is very friendly and playful.

▼ **A very agile animal.** The rock wallaby uses its flexible tail to move with ease around the dangerous rocky terrain it inhabits.

Olympic jumps. The kangaroo's long-jump record stands at over 36 feet (11 m). This is much longer than any Olympic athlete.

Living fossils. The marsupial wolf was thought to have died out in 1933. But recent studies seem to show there are still a few specimens in Australia.

▼ Hunting at night.

Kangaroos spend most of the day resting in the shade. They start to become more active in the afternoon, and nighttime is when they carry out most of their activities. This is the best way to avoid the suffocating daytime heat.

1. Kangaroos belong to the family:
a) Cangurid.
b) Macropodidae.
a) Saltorid.

2. Joeys leave the pouch:
a) at five days.
b) at two years.
c) between 190 and 200 days.

3. How fast can a kangaroo move?
a) 30 miles (50 km) per hour.
b) 18 miles (30 km) per hour.
c) 62 miles (100 km) per hour.

4. Kangaroos can jump:
a) 10 feet (3 m) long.
b) 23 feet (7 m) long.
c) over 30 feet (9 m) long.

5. The Tasmanian devil is:
a) extinct.
b) a kangaroo ancestor.
c) found only in Tasmania.

6. An opossum is:
a) a North American marsupial.
b) a species of mole.
c) the shape of a kangaroo's foot.

The answers to KANGAROO SECRETS questions are on page 32.

GLOSSARY

abdomen: the section of the body that contains the digestive organs.

agile: nimble; able to move quickly or easily.

ancestors: previous generations.

canine teeth: sharp, pointed teeth in front of an animal's mouth, used for tearing off pieces of meat or other tough food.

carnivores: meat-eating animals.

compete: oppose; to come into conflict with.

continents: the large landmasses of Earth, which include Africa, Antarctica, Asia, Australia, Europe, North America, and South America.

diversify: to increase the variety of; to take part in various activities.

drought: a long period of time with very little or no rain.

emu: a large Australian bird that looks like an ostrich.

esophagus: the tube inside the body that connects the throat to the stomach so food can pass into it.

evolution: changing or developing gradually from one form to another. Over time, all living things evolve to survive in their changing environments, or they may become extinct. Most of today's life-forms, including humans, evolved from ancestors that may have looked and behaved quite differently. Scientists learn more about how organisms develop by studying how they once were or what their ancestors were like through fossils.

extinct: no longer in existence.

fetus: an unborn baby.

flexible: able to bend or move with ease.

flora: the plant life in a particular area or region.

fossils: the remains, impression, or traces of an animal or plant from an earlier time period that are often found in rock or in Earth's crust.

gestation: the period of time in the reproductive cycle between conception and birth.

habitat: the natural home of a plant or animal.

herbivores: animals that eat only plants.

incisors: sharp teeth at the front of an animal's mouth that are used for cutting.

inhabit: to live in or on.

isolation: the condition of being set apart from others; alone.

mammals: warm-blooded animals that have backbones, hair, give birth to live young, and produce milk to feed them.

marsupials: animals, such as kangaroos and opossums, that carry their newborn young in pouches located on the outside of the mother's body.

mate (*v*): to join together (animals) to produce young; to breed a male and a female.

nurture: to care for; to nourish.

offspring: the young of an animal or plant.

pouch: a part of an animal's body that is like a bag. The female kangaroo has a pouch, also called a marsupium, on the outside of its body. This pouch is used to transport, or carry, the kangaroo's young.

predators: animals that kill and eat other animals.

prey: animals that are hunted, captured, and killed for food by other animals.

quadruped: an animal with four feet.

remote: far from main traffic routes.

rival: someone or something that is against another in a fight or contest.

roam: to wander aimlessly; to move around without a specific purpose.

snout: protruding nose and jaw of an animal.

species: animals or plants that are closely related and often similar in behavior and appearance. Members of the same species are able to breed together.

subspecies: a classification just under species of an isolated group that is different in shape or function from a species. Different subspecies of the same species can breed together.

suckle: to nurse; to draw milk from the mother's breast.

terrain: the physical features of a piece of land.

Tertiary period: the geologic time period when mountains began to form and when mammals dominated the land.

troop: a group of kangaroos that lives and travels together.

tropical: belonging to the tropics, or the region centered on the equator and lying between the Tropic of Cancer (23.5 degrees north of the equator) and the Tropic of Capricorn (23.5 degrees south of the equator). This region is typically very hot and humid.

uterus: that part of a mother's body where a baby is conceived and carried until birth.

ACTIVITIES

◆ Kangaroos are marsupials. Find some books at the library that tell what other marsupials are similar to kangaroos. How are marsupials different from placental mammals?

◆ In a notebook, write down some facts about the climate and vegetation of Australia that you find in library books or nature magazines, such as *National Geographic*. How are kangaroos able to survive in Australia's climate? Do other Australian marsupials have similar ways of surviving?

◆ Long ago, South America was home to many types of marsupials. Do some research in a library to find out what kinds of marsupials once lived in South America. These animals became extinct after a land bridge connected North America and South America. Can you think why this happened? What animals crossed this bridge, and what effect did they have on the local animal population?

MORE BOOKS TO READ

A First Look at Kangaroos, Koalas, and Other Animals with Pouches.
    Millicent E. Selsam and Joyce Hunt (Walker)
A Picture Book of Australian Animals. Kellie Conforth
    (Troll Communications)
Kangaroo. Caroline Arnold (Morrow Jr. Books)
Kangaroos. Emilie Lepthien (Childrens)
Kangaroos. Kate Petty (Barron)
Kangaroos. William R. Sanford and Carl R. Green (Silver Burdett)
Kangaroos on Location. Kathy Darling (Lothrop)
Kelly the Kangaroo. Bob Storms (Heian International)
Pocket Babies. Katherine M. Marko (Watts)

VIDEOS

The Kangaroos. (Centre Communications)
Kangaroos and Wallabies. (Rainbow Educational Media)
Valley of the Kangaroos. (National Geographic Society)
The Wonderful Kangaroo. (Wood Knapp Video)
Wonders Down Under. (Library Video)

PLACES TO VISIT

Oklahoma City Zoological Park
2101 Northeast 50th Street
Oklahoma City, OK 73111

Metro Toronto Zoo
Meadowvale Road
West Hill
Toronto, ON M1E 4R5

Perth Zoological Gardens
South Perth, Australia

Philadelphia Zoological Garden
In Fairmount Park
34th Street and Girard
    Avenue
Philadelphia, PA 19104

Royal Melbourne Zoological Gardens
Elliott Avenue
Parkville, Victoria
Australia 3052

Wellington Zoo
Newtown, New Zealand

Calgary Zoo
1300 Zoo Road
Calgary, AB T2V 7E6

Indianapolis Zoo
1200 West Washington
    Street
Indianapolis, IN 46222

INDEX

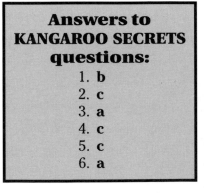

Answers to KANGAROO SECRETS questions:
1. **b**
2. **c**
3. **a**
4. **c**
5. **c**
6. **a**